Pigs on a Farm

Abbie Mercer

PowerKiDS press.
New York

For mon père et tous mes petits cochons

Published in 2010 by The Rosen Publishing Group, Inc.
29 East 21st Street, New York, NY 10010

First Edition

Editor: Amelie von Zumbusch
Book Design: Kate Laczynski
Photo Researcher: Jessica Gerweck

Photo Credits: Cover, pp. 1, 5, 7, 9, 11, 13, 15, 17, 19, 21, 24 Shutterstock.com; p. 23 © www.istockphoto.com/Rhoberazzi.

Library of Congress Cataloging-in-Publication Data

Mercer, Abbie.
  Pigs on a farm / Abbie Mercer. — 1st ed.
      p. cm. — (Barnyard animals)
  Includes index.
  ISBN 978-1-4042-8053-3 (library binding) — ISBN 978-1-4042-8067-0 (pbk.) — ISBN 978-1-4042-8068-7 (6-pack)
  1. Swine—Juvenile literature. I. Title. II. Series.
  SF395.5.M47 2010
  636.4—dc22   **3 1561 00227 0118**
                              2008051546

Manufactured in the United States of America

Contents

Pigs are smart animals. They learn easily and quickly.

Pigs live on farms. On small farms, pigs live in **pigsties**.

Pigs that live on pig farms most often live in big barns.

Pigs can be several colors, such as pink, black, or brown. Some pigs are a mix of colors.

Pigs have round noses, called **snouts**. Pigs have a very good sense of smell.

13

Male pigs are called boars, while females are known as sows. Baby pigs are **piglets**.

Piglets like to play and nap. They drink their mothers' milk and grow quickly.

As they grow older, pigs eat many foods. Farmers feed pigs mostly **grain**.

When they are outside, pigs can find their own food. They eat many foods, such as roots, nuts, and fruit.

On hot days, pigs roll in mud to cool off. The mud also helps keep bugs away.

Words to Know

grain

piglets

pigsty

snout

Index

Web Sites

Due to the changing nature of Internet links, PowerKids Press has developed an online list of Web sites related to the subject of this book. This site is updated regularly. Please use this link to access the list: www.powerkidslinks.com/byard/pigs/